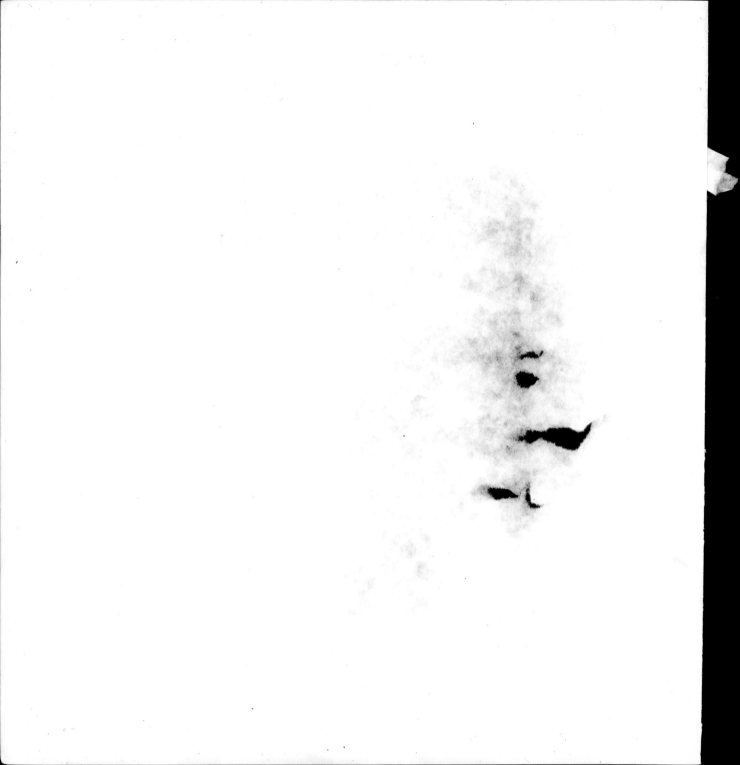

El Salvador

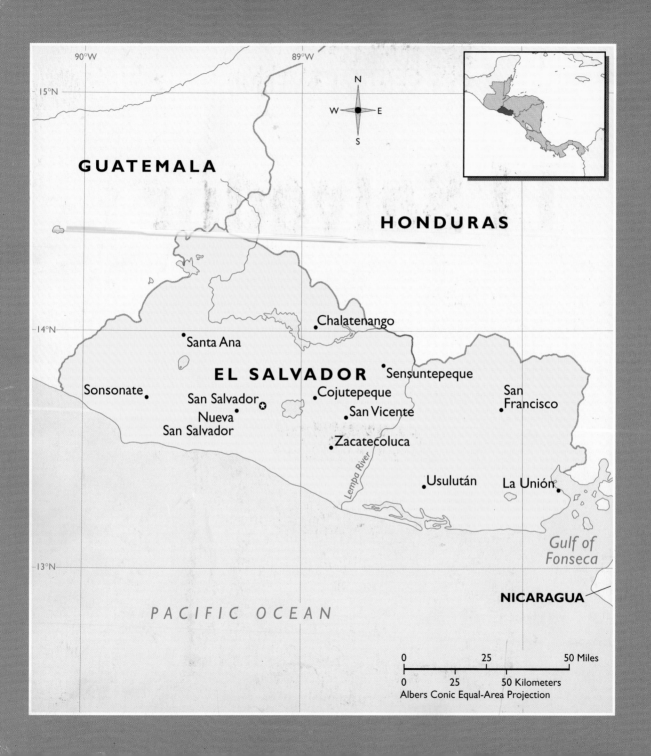

GUATEMALA

HONDURAS

15°N

90°W   89°W

N
W   E
S

EL SALVADOR

14°N

• Chalatenango

• Santa Ana

• Sensuntepeque

Sonsonate
•

San Salvador
•
Nueva
San Salvador
•

☆

• Cojutepeque
San Vicente
•

San
Francisco
•

Zacatecoluca
•

Lempa River

• Usulután

La Unión
•

13°N

Gulf of
Fonseca

PACIFIC OCEAN

NICARAGUA

0   25   50 Miles

0   25   50 Kilometers
Albers Conic Equal-Area Projection

DISCOVERING
CENTRAL AMERICA

El Salvador

Charles J. Shields

Mason Crest Publishers
Philadelphia

Mason Crest Publishers
370 Reed Road
Broomall PA 19008
www.masoncrest.com

First printing

1 3 5 7 9 8 6 4 2

Library of Congress Cataloging-in-Publication Data
on file at the Library of Congress

ISBN 1-59084-094-1

**DISCOVERING
CENTRAL AMERICA**

Belize   **Guatemala**
Central America: Facts and Figures   **Honduras**
Costa Rica   **Nicaragua**
El Salvador   **Panama**

Discovering Central America

James D. Henderson

CENTRAL AMERICA is a beautiful part of the world, filled with generous and friendly people. It is also a region steeped in history, one of the first areas of the New World explored by Christopher Columbus. Central America is both close to the United States and strategically important to it. For nearly a century ships of the U.S. and the world have made good use of the Panama Canal. And for longer than that breakfast tables have been graced by the bananas and other tropical fruits that Central America produces in abundance.

Central America is closer to North America and other peoples of the world with each passing day. Globalized trade brings the region's products to world markets as never before. And there is promise that trade agreements will soon unite all nations of the Americas in a great common market. Meanwhile improved road and air links make it easy for visitors to reach Middle America. Central America's tropical flora and fauna are ever more accessible to foreign visitors having an interest in eco-tourism. Other visitors are drawn to the region's dazzling Pacific Ocean beaches, jewel-like scenery, and bustling towns and cities. And everywhere Central America's wonderful and varied peoples are outgoing and welcoming to foreign visitors.

These eight books are intended to provide complete, up-to-date information on the five countries historians call Central America (Guatemala, El Salvador, Honduras, Nicaragua, Costa Rica), as well as on Panama (technically part of South America) and Belize (technically part of North America). Each volume contains chapters on the land, history, economy, people, and cultures of the countries treated. And each country study is written in an engaging style, employing a vocabulary appropriate to young students.

A worker pauses between the trees on a coffee plantation in San Salvador.

All volumes contain colorful illustrations, maps, and up-to-date boxed information of a statistical character, and each is accompanied by a chronology, a glossary, a bibliography, selected Internet resources, and an index. Students and teachers alike will welcome the many suggestions for individual and class projects and reports contained in each country study, and they will want to prepare the tasty traditional dishes described in each volume's recipe section.

This eight-book series is a timely and useful addition to the literature on Central America. It is designed not just to inform, but also to engage school-aged readers with this important and fascinating part of the Americas.

Let me introduce this series as author Charles J. Shields begins each volume: *¡Hola!* You are discovering Central America!

El Salvador has been an unstable land both politically and geographically. In January 2001 a mud slide (opposite) wiped out homes in Santa Tecia, killing many people. In the same month, scientists reported that volcanic activity within Ilamatepec (right), a volcano in Santa Ana about 50 miles from the country's capital, has intensified.

1 A Small, Struggling Land

¡HOLA! ARE YOU DISCOVERING the Republic of El Salvador? El Salvador is a tropical land of mountains, cone-shaped volcanoes, green valleys, and scenic lakes, surrounded by cloud-misted hills. Unfortunately, however, El Salvador has also suffered repeatedly from natural *catastrophes*. Earthquakes have badly damaged or destroyed the city of San Salvador 14 times. Hurricanes are rare, but severe *droughts* have caused widespread losses. On top of this, civil war tore El Salvador apart in the 1980s. As one travel writer put it, "Unlike its neighbors, El Salvador is not geared to independent travelers. What it does offer is a whole new experience of watching a country strive to redefine itself."

Quick Facts: The Geography of El Salvador

Location: Middle America, bordering the northern Pacific Ocean, between Guatemala and Honduras.

Geographic coordinates: 13'50" N, 88'55" W

Area: (slightly smaller than Massachusetts)
total: 21,040 sq. km
land: 20,720 sq. km
water: 320 sq. km

Borders: Guatemala 203 km; Honduras 342 km; coastline: 307 km.

Climate: tropical; rainy season (May to October); dry season (November to April); tropical on coast; temperate in uplands.

Terrain: mostly mountains with narrow coastal belt and central plateau.

Elevation extremes:
lowest point: Pacific Ocean 0 m
highest point: Cerro El Pital 2,730 m

Natural resources: hydropower, geothermal power, petroleum, arable land.

Land use:
arable land: 27 percent
permanent crops: 8 percent
permanent pastures: 29 percent
forests and woodland: 5 percent
other: 31 percent
Irrigated land: 1,200 sq. km

Small, but Populous

Lying on the western side of the Central American *isthmus*, El Salvador is the only Central American nation without a Caribbean coast. The Pacific Ocean lies to its south, Guatemala to its northwest, and Honduras to its northeast. Also, with a total area of 8,123 square miles (21,041 square kilometers), El Salvador is the smallest of the seven Central American countries. Shaped like a rectangle, it is slightly smaller in area than the state of Massachusetts. In population, however, it is the third largest Central American country and the most densely populated.

Because it is such a small nation, El Salvador lacks a wide range of natural resources. Most of the inhabited country is on a fertile volcanic *plateau* about 2,000 feet (607 meters) high. In addition, because El Salvador is without major mountains to influence the weather, there are few variations in rainfall and temperature.

Three Distinct Landscapes

Three distinct landscapes extend east to west across the country: the Coastal Lowlands, the Central Region, and the Interior Highlands.

The Coastal Lowlands—a 10- to 12-mile-wide (16- to 19-km) coastal plain—parallels the Pacific Ocean, interrupted only by volcanic hills. Large sections of the land have been developed for farming. Many factories and a fishing industry are located near Acajutla, the leading port.

A row of volcanoes separates the Coastal Lowlands from a second landscape—narrow interior valleys known as the Central Region. The Central Region forms the heartland of El Salvador.

About three-fourths of the nation's people live in the Central Region, many in such large cities as San Salvador (population 422,600) and Santa Ana (population 202,300). Most of the country's industry and fertile farm-land is here, too. The southern border of this region, the Coastal Range, is a band of rugged mountains and high, inactive volcanoes. On the range's lower slopes, coffee *plantations* and cattle ranches are interspersed among forests of oak and pine trees. A broad, deeply eroded plateau of gently rolling land lies north of the Coastal Range. The plateau's volcanic soil and green pastures make it El Salvador's chief agricultural region. Although two peaks in the row of volcanoes and several peaks in the volcanic plateau near the Honduran border reach 7,000 feet (2,134 m), very little of the land surface in El Salvador is higher than 5,000 feet (1,524 m) in elevation.

The Interior Highlands occupy northern El Salvador and make up the most thinly populated region of the country. The Sierra Madre—a low mountain range of hardened lava, rocks, and volcanic ash—covers most of the highlands. Only a few small farms and ranches are located in the Interior Highlands.

El Salvador's largest river, the Lempa, starts in the Sierra Madre of the Interior Highlands. A major source of hydroelectric power, it drains the northwestern part of the country. Taking a course southward midway across the country, the Lempa cuts across an interior valley, the row of volcanoes, and the coastal plain before emptying into the Pacific Ocean, 200 miles (320 km) from its beginning. El Salvador also has three large lakes: Lake Guija, Lake Coatepeque, and Lake Ilopango.

In total, nearly 150 rivers flow through El Salvador to the Pacific Ocean. Many of the country's rivers, however, suffer from pollution. Some observers fear that at the current rate of destruction, the country will run out of drinking water in less than 15 years. El Salvador is the only country in Latin America without environmental protection laws.

Volcanoes and Earthquakes

El Salvador is dotted with more than 25 extinct volcanoes, many with craters showing ancient lava flows. Three other volcanoes are considered only "at rest" because they have shown little activity, but they do occasionally belch sulfur fumes. These volcanoes are San Miguel, Santa Ana, and Izalco.

El Salvador is located in an unstable *geological* zone and suffers frequent earthquakes. Far beneath the ground, gigantic *tectonic* plates collide with one another, triggering the shocks. An powerful earthquake with a *magnitude* of 7.6 on the *Richter scale* struck El Salvador in January 2001, resulting in the deaths of more than 700 people. The following month, a 6.1-magnitude earthquake killed over 275 more people.

Two Seasons

El Salvador has a tropical climate that varies slightly from area to area and only because of differences in altitude. Average year-round temperatures range from 80° F (27° C) in Acajutla along the coast to 73° F (23° C) in Santa Ana in the mountains.

Because of El Salvador's location, it is frequently shaken by earthquakes. These homes in the village of San Miguel Tepezonte were destroyed by a strong earthquake in February 2001 that killed more than 275 people.

The sun sets over the El Jocotal lagoon in El Salvador. To protect the many types of animals and plants native to El Salvador, the lagoon has been made a nature preserve.

There are two distinct seasons in El Salvador. The dry season occurs from November to April, with light rainfall. During the rainy season, from May to October, showers fall every afternoon. Rainfall is heaviest along the coast. The interior regions remain relatively dry. Average monthly rainfall during the wet season is 10 inches. Yearly rainfall ranges from 85 inches total along the coast to less than 60 inches in the northwest.

Plants and Animals

Because El Salvador does not face the Caribbean Sea, it has the least number of tropical plants among Central American countries. The weather is not as warm and humid on the Pacific side as it is on the Caribbean side; therefore, El Salvador does not have the lush, varied *vegetation* usually associated with Central American countries. Moreover, the native vegetation is scarce because most of the woods and forest have disappeared, replaced by farms, ranches, and plantations that produce grains, beef, sugar cane, and cotton. But there still exists lush and colorful vegetation in some places. More than 200 different species of orchid, for example, grow all over the country.

Another result of so much destruction of the native vegetation is that some animals are endangered now—crested eagles and jaguars, for example. In order to avoid and restore this damage, El Salvador has established *preserves*. Among the largest are Montecristo Cloud Forest, El Impossible Woods, Cerro Verde National Park, Deininger National Park, and El Jocotal Lagoon.

Over 400 different bird species can be found in El Salvador—17 hummingbird species are located in Cerro Verde National Park alone. El Salvador is a true delight for the bird watcher!

(Opposite) Activist members of the Farabundo Martí Liberation Front (FMLN) take part in a convention to name a presidential candidate in 1998. The FMLN was involved in the civil war that divided El Salvador during the 1980s. (Right) Jose Napoleon Duarte answers reporters' questions. Duarte was the leader of a reform movement in the country during the early 1970s.

2 A History of Struggle

THE NAME EL SALVADOR, given to the land by Spanish conquerors, comes from the Roman Catholic feast of San Salvador del Mundo (Holy Savior of the World). Yet El Salvador's history has not been peaceful. Many people remember El Salvador as the scene of a brutal civil war fought throughout the 1980s. Today, international relief organizations are helping to rebuild El Salvador with programs for education, agriculture, reforestation, human rights, and health care.

"Land of Precious Things"

Traces of El Salvador's civilization date back to 1500 B.C. By A.D. 1000, two large Amerindian states and several smaller ones flourished in the region, mainly populated by the Pipils. The Pipils were a tribe of *nomadic* people whose culture was like the Aztec's, except they had done away with human sacrifice. Ruins belonging to the Pipils lie scattered throughout present-day El Salvador.

On May 31, 1522, a Spanish ship's officer named Andres Niño led an expedition to the shore of Meanguera Island, located in the Gulf of Fonseca. This was the first visit by the Spanish to the Salvadoran coast. Two years later, in June 1524, Spanish captain Pedro de Alvarado arrived, prepared for conquest. For 30 days, de Alvarado's troops fought the tribes of the country, which was then called by the Amerindians "Cuzcatlan," meaning "Land of Precious Things." Hundreds, perhaps thousands, of Amerindians were killed, but de Alvarado was driven off. He returned the following year, and this time he succeeded in conquering the tribes.

Spanish rule lasted three centuries. During that period, El Salvador was a *province* of Spain's kingdom of Guatemala. In 1811, a brief revolution against Spanish rule flared up inside El Salvador. This revolt failed. In 1821, however, all the Central American countries freed themselves from Spain, declaring their independence.

For a brief time, El Salvador was part of a *federation* of Central American states until that union ended in 1838. For decades after, El Salvador struggled with revolutions inside its own borders and with wars against other Central American republics.

Did You Know?

El Salvador's flag consists of three equal horizontal bands of blue (top), white, and blue with the national coat of arms centered in the white band. The coat of arms features a round emblem encircled by the words "Republica De El Salvador En La America Central."

Military Rule

El Salvador experienced a long period of stability from 1900 to 1930. Then, in 1932, the military succeeded in toppling the government, crushing protest throughout the countryside. Over the years, until 1980, all but one Salvadoran president was an army officer. Elections were seldom fair.

During the years of military rule, wealthy landowners vigorously supported the government. From their point of view, the balance in the power structure was ideal. The military ensured peace, so the prosperous coffee-growing families could continue doing business without interruption. The entire economy suffered, however, when coffee prices dropped.

In addition, a serious social problem was boiling beneath the surface. As the supply of available land became exhausted, many Salvadorans moved from the countryside to the cities, beginning in the 1940s. About 300,000 other Salvadorans spilled over the border into Honduras, illegally seizing open

The archbishop of San Salvador during the 1970s, Oscar Arnulfo Romero, was a social advocate. He demanded equality and justice for the poor of El Salvador, and denounced the violence that threatened to tear the country apart. In March 1980 he was nominated for the Nobel Peace Prize because of his message on social issues. That same month, on March 24, he was shot to death while conducting mass.

land. In July 1969, El Salvador and Honduras fought each other in the 100-hour Soccer War, which erupted over border disputes. (The conflict was called the Soccer War because the two countries happened to be facing each other in a series of championship soccer matches at the time.) The two combatants formally signed a peace treaty on October 30, 1980, which put the dispute before the International Court of Justice. In September 1992, the court issued a 400-page ruling, awarding much of the land in question to Honduras.

During the 1970s, many people in El Salvador were unhappy about the country's social problems, poor economy, and repressive dictatorship. In the 1972 presidential election, the opponents of military rule united under

Jose Napoleon Duarte, leader of the Christian Democratic Party (PDC). Duarte was defeated by widespread fraud at the polls, and later went into *exile*. With Duarte and his promises of democratic *reforms* now gone, armed groups rose up to bring about democratic change by force.

Alvaro Magaña speaks on the American television program *Face the Nation* in June 1982. Magaña had been selected as El Salvador's temporary president while a new constitution was being written in 1982–83.

By 1979, *guerrilla* warfare, led by the Farabundo Martí National Liberation Front (FMLN), was widespread throughout the country. About 1 million Salvadorans—one-fifth of the population—fled to neighboring Central American countries and the United States. Hundreds of thousands more sought safety by crowding into El Salvador's cities. Both the guerrillas and the poorly trained Salvadoran armed forces terrorized the population with random killings. The United States, believing the best hope for peace lay with the government, sided with the Salvadoran military.

The Beginnings of Democracy

On October 15, 1979, reform-minded military officers and civilian leaders overthrew the government, and Duarte returned from exile. Under his leadership, land belonging to wealthy families was divided up, banks were brought under government control, and political parties were allowed to function again. On March 28, 1982, Salvadorans elected a new assembly. Following the election, the assembly peacefully transferred power to a temporary president whom they had selected—Alvaro Magaña.

The 1983 constitution, drafted by the assembly, strengthened individual rights, established safeguards against being imprisoned illegally and unreasonable searches, and established a *republican* form of government. It also advanced the rights of farm and plantation workers. In 1984, Duarte won the presidential election, becoming the first freely elected president in 50 years. The reforms did not satisfy the FMLN, however. Generally, their leaders demanded a more *communistic* society. In 1989, Alfredo Cristiani won the presidential election with 54 percent of the vote—the first time that

Francisco Flores Perez, the president of El Salvador, gives a speech on implementing a broad plan to combat violence in San Salvador. Flores was 39 years old when he was elected president in June 1999, making him the youngest president elected in El Salvador.

power had passed peacefully from one freely elected civilian leader to another in El Salvador. Cristiani called for direct talks to end the decades of conflict between the government and guerrillas. The talks broke down in September 1989, when guerrillas launched a bloody, nationwide attack.

An End to the Civil War

At the request of other Central American presidents, the United Nations became involved in trying to end El Salvador's civil war. After a year of little progress, the government and the FMLN accepted an invitation from the United Nations to meet in New York City. On September 25, 1991, the two sides signed the New York City Accord. On December 31, 1991, the government and the FMLN signed a second, more detailed peace agreement. The final agreement, called the Accords of

Chapultepec, was signed in Mexico City on January 16, 1992. A nine-month cease-fire took effect February 1, 1992, and has never been broken.

During the 12-year civil war, 75,000 lives were lost and the economy of El Salvador was heavily damaged. To try to help its economy, El Salvador, together with Guatemala and Honduras, signed a *free trade* agreement with Mexico in June 2000. President Francisco Flores Perez also won approval for a U.S. military base in El Salvador, despite protests from former rebels who feared U.S. control over El Salvador's affairs. The base fights drug trafficking in the region and replaces a military base that was closed in Panama when the United States returned control of the Panama Canal to Panama in 1999. Currently, dozens of foreign aid groups work closely with the Salvadoran government to improve living conditions in El Salvador.

ENDA Y MOLINO

SE VENDE
HYELO
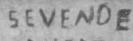

(Opposite) A variety of fruits are available at this grocery shop in San Vicente. (Right) A worker at a sugar cane factory in San Salvador pours molasses into large vats for transportation. Since the end of the civil war, El Salvador's economy has been growing stronger.

3 A Changing Economy

EL SALVADOR IS a poor Central American country that suffers from a weak tax collection system, the aftermath of Hurricane Mitch, and low world-coffee prices. In addition, the long-term impact of the civil war on El Salvador's economy was devastating. On the bright side, in recent years, total *exports* have grown steadily. In addition, El Salvador's economy is growing stronger from money sent home by Salvadorans living abroad and from aid provided by world relief organizations and foreign nations.

Rich Soil, Weak Economy

El Salvador's chief natural resource is its fertile volcanic soil, which is ideal for growing crops such as coffee. For more than 100 years, coffee farming has been the center of the economy of El Salvador. As a crop, coffee was introduced in El Salvador in the 1850s. It was so successful that by 1870 it had replaced the dye *indigo* as the nation's major export. Between 1900 and the early 1940s, coffee made up about 90 percent, and never less than 75 percent, of Salvadoran exports. Coffee growing has been the major source of employment and has paid for the cost of governments and the construction of highways, railroads, and ports. Village lands were turned into coffee estates on which peasants worked. Coffee growers and the military became the rulers of El Salvador.

After World War II, Salvadoran planters made a move to rely less on coffee because a drop in prices meant financial disaster. Woodlands and natural pastures on the coastal plain were turned into cotton or sugar cane farms. Cotton and sugar cane thrive in the warm, humid lowlands. Export of these products has been increasing since the 1960s.

Today, El Salvador's economy still depends mainly on agriculture. Cropland and pastures cover three-fourths of the country, and over half of all workers are farmers or ranchers. The ranchers raise beef and dairy cattle. Farmers—many of them working small plots—raise beans, corn, rice, and other crops for their families and for local markets. Other farmers work on large commercial plantations called *fincas*, growing coffee, cotton, and sugar cane. El Salvador is also the only producer in the world of balsa, a woody plant used in medicines and cosmetics. (Balsa strips can also be found in U.S. hobby stores, as they are used to make models).

With El Salvador being as small as it is, more land for additional commercial agriculture is scarce. In fact, there are no unoccupied lands at all for poor farmers, who raise *subsistence* crops of corn, beans, and *sorghum*. These farmers make up 40 percent of the population. El Salvador's government continues to encourage new industries so that the country will depend less on agriculture. Even so, manufacturing and industry still account for only a small percentage of El Salvador's national income.

Land Reform

Before 1980, a small but wealthy group of Salvadorans owned most of the land in El Salvador and controlled agriculture by themselves. About 70 percent of the farmers at this time rented land or worked on large plantations but lived in poverty.

The civilian-military *junta* that came to power in 1979 enacted a far-reaching land reform program. The goal was to secure peace and prosperity for more Salvadorans by developing a middle class of farmers. More than 22 percent of El Salvador's total farmland was transferred to those who worked the land but did not own it, benefit-

A child harvests coffee beans. Coffee has been one of El Salvador's most important export crops for more than 150 years.

ing at least 525,000 people. Nevertheless, by 1990, when land reform ended, about 150,000 landless families remained. The United States provided $300 million for a national reconstruction plan, including $60 million for land purchases. In addition, U.S.-funded agencies continue to provide technical training, farm loans, and other financial services.

Manufacturing and Industry

Salvadorans have a reputation for being hard working. Historically, El Salvador has been the most industrialized nation in Central America.

Textiles, food processing, and the manufacture of shoes, clothing, and pharmaceuticals are leading industries. Manufacturing increased suddenly during the 1960s after the establishment of the Central American Common Market. The arrangement eased trade barriers between member nations of the region. Today, manufacturing accounts for about 22 percent of the total value of goods and services produced in the country each year.

Since 1993, industry in El Salvador has expanded by using "free zones." Wholesalers

A worker harvests cotton in El Salvador. Over the past five decades, cotton has become a more important part of El Salvador's economy.

and retailers from abroad locate in free zones because they can bring in container loads of goods and break them down into smaller shipments for resale. Or, they can assemble goods from abroad for re-export. In a sense, a free zone is like a giant discount warehouse with no taxes added to sales. Local people benefit from the creation of jobs in free zones. Furthermore, exports leaving El Salvador's free zones have made an important contribution to its economy.

Trade

Exports have expanded since World War II from the rise of manufacturing and an increase in cotton and sugar cane sales. Nevertheless, coffee continues to make up half of all sales abroad. The agricultural products are sent primarily to Western Europe, the United States, and Japan. Manufactured products are exported to neighboring countries of Central America.

Imports come primarily from the United States, Central America, Europe, and Venezuela. They consist of petroleum, textiles, food products, chemicals, machinery, and transport equipment.

United States' support for El Salvador's private electrical and telecommunications markets has attracted U.S. investment in the country. Over 300 U.S. companies have businesses or offices in El Salvador.

Best System of Railroads and Highways

El Salvador has the best system of railroads and highways in Central America because much of the land is flat and regular. Railroads for carrying

Quick Facts: The Economy of Nicaragua

Per capita income (2001): $3,100; 48 percent of the population lives below the poverty line.

Industry (22 percent of GDP*): Food and beverage processing, textiles, footwear and clothing, chemical products, petroleum products, electronics.

Agriculture (12 percent of GDP): coffee, sugar cane, corn, rice, beans, oilseed, cotton, sorghum, beef, dairy products, shrimp.

Services (66 percent of GDP): government services, finance.

Foreign trade (2001): Exports $2.5 billion: coffee, sugar, textiles, shrimp.

Major markets: United States, 64 percent; Central American Common Market (CACM), 25 percent; European Union (EU), 4 percent; others, 7 percent.

Labor force by occupation (1999): agriculture, 30 percent; industry, 15 percent; services, 55 percent.

Unemployment rate: 7.7 percent.

Economic growth rate: 2.2 percent.

Currency exchange rate: 8.75 Salvadoran colones = U.S. $1.

* GDP or gross domestic product—the total value of goods and services produced in a year

coffee to the ports of Acajutla and La Unión were built in the 1880s. In 1927, a railroad was completed through Guatemala to the Caribbean coast so coffee could be shipped directly to Europe and the southeastern United States.

El Salvador also has a good network of highways. The Inter-American Highway passes through the interior valley, with links to the coastal highway and to the seaports on the Pacific. But fewer than two percent of all Salvadorans own an automobile. Most people travel by bus.

Effects of Hurricane Mitch

Hurricane Mitch struck El Salvador in late October 1998, flooding thousands of acres of farmland and killing 374 people. In addition, 55,864 people were left homeless. Three major bridges that cross the Lempa were swept away, isolating part of the country. Heavy rainfall, flooding, and mudslides also damaged El Salvador's network of roads. Unclean water and poor sanitation created health problems. The Ministry of Health recorded a total of 109,038 medical cases related to Hurricane Mitch between October 31 and November 18, 1998. Most were respiratory infections, skin ailments, diarrhea, and eye infections.

Sixteen foreign governments, including the United States, and dozens of international relief agencies provided El Salvador with assistance. The government of El Salvador reported that 961 tons of goods and food were received. The Ministry of Foreign Affairs estimated that contributions in cash given directly to the Salvadoran government totaled $4.3 million.

The Biggest Challenge

Maintaining a steady economy has been the biggest challenge to El Salvador in recent years. Fortunately, El Salvador's debt decreased sharply in 1993, chiefly as a result of an agreement under which the United States forgave about $461 million of official debt.

El Salvador also relies on donations from abroad. Large amounts of money come in through private organizations, such as political parties, unions, and churches. Donors have pledged $1.26 billion over the next several years to finance El Salvador's reconstruction and modernization efforts.

In January 2001, the U.S. dollar became the legal currency in El Salvador, which plans to gradually phase out its own coins and bills as a cost-saving measure.

(Opposite) A young boy cuts sugar cane in a field near San Lorenzo.
(Right) A Salvadoran girl stands in front of tents at the shelter camp in Las Delicias. She and her family were left homeless after a major earthquake in January 2001, which destroyed about 46,000 homes and killed more than 700 people.

4 The Most Crowded Country in Central America

CURRENTLY, EL SALVADOR'S population numbers about 6.2 million. They are squeezed into a country of just over 13,000 square miles, making El Salvador the most crowded country in Central America.

Almost 90 percent of El Salvador's population are of mixed Indian and Spanish descent. Nine percent are white, mostly Spanish. Other ethnic groups include the Lebanese, Swiss, Turks, Syrians, Germans, and Chinese. Only about 1 percent are Amerindian, and very few still observe Amerindian customs and traditions. Nearly all Salvadorans speak Spanish, and most are Roman Catholic, although Protestant groups are growing. About 1.7 million people live in the capital, San Salvador, but almost half of El Salvador's population lives in the countryside.

Mostly Mestizo

By far, the majority of Salvadorans are *mestizos*—persons of mixed Spanish and Amerindian descent. When the Spanish entered the region that became El Salvador, a dense population of Amerindians lived there. Following the Spanish conquest, though, the **conquistadors** managed to settle throughout the territory because the land was open and easily occupied.

As a result, Europeans and natives lived together, and Amerindians gradually adapted many European customs. Today, remaining Amerindians in El Salvador make up only a fraction of the population. They are mostly descended from the Pipil Indians—the dominant tribe in the area when the Spanish conquerors arrived. The Pipil live mainly in the southwestern highlands near the Guatemalan border. A few Indians still speak the ancient Nahuatl language of the Pipils and follow the traditional ways of life of the tribe.

The Densest Population

El Salvador ranks as the most densely populated nation on the mainland of the Americas. There were 800,000 people in El Salvador in 1900. The number increased to 1.6 million by 1940, and to about 6.2 million in 2002. The density of the population is 644 persons per square mile (249 per sq. km)— 10 times as many people per square mile as the United States, which has the largest population in the Americas. By comparison to its Central American neighbors, El Salvador is three-and-a-half times more dense than Guatemala, and up to 10 times more dense than other Central American nations.

Because of the high density, many

A woman carries her belongings through a street in Suchitoto. Outside of the cities, living conditions are poor for many Salvadorans.

Quick Facts: The People of El Salvador

Population: 6,122,515

Ethnic groups: 90 percent *mestizo*; 9 percent white; 1 percent Amerindian.

Age structure:
0–14 years: 38 percent
15–64 years: 57 percent
65 years and over: 5 percent

Population growth rate: 1.87 percent

Birth rate: 29.02 births/1,000 population

Infant mortality rate: 29.22 deaths/1,000 live births

Death rate: 6.27 deaths/1,000 population

Life expectancy at birth:
total population: 69.74 years
male: 66.14 years
female: 73.52 years

Total fertility rate: 3.38 children born per woman.

Religions: 86 percent Roman Catholic; 7.5 percent Protestant; 6.5 percent other.

Languages: Spanish, Nahuatl (among some Amerindians).

Literacy: 71.5 percent

*All figures 2002 estimates, unless otherwise noted.

Salvadorans have migrated to less populated areas in surrounding countries. Ownership of scarce fertile land—El Salvador's main resource—has been a cause of turmoil and conflict in the country.

Urban and Rural Housing

The number of persons living in towns and cities versus the country-side is about equal. El Salvador's population tends to be concentrated in the Coastal Lowlands and the Central Region. The three largest cities—San Salvador, Santa Ana, and San Miguel—lie in basins at the feet of volcanoes.

Housing outside the cities is modest, and in some cases, barely livable. Some farmers own adobe houses with dirt floors and thatched roofs made of straw or palm leaves. Poorer people in the countryside live in huts made of wattle walls—interwoven branches smeared with mud. The wealthy in El Salvador live in modern homes.

Poor people tend to crowd the cities in the hope of finding work. Most are forced to rent one-room apartments in decaying *slums*. Middle-class city dwellers live in row houses—brick buildings sharing a common wall between them—or in better apartments. The rich live in suburbs, where modern homes with yards often have gardens.

Inadequate Schools

Although El Salvador's system of public education is substandard, a majority of El Salvador's adults can read and write. In poor rural areas, though, more than half of the children of elementary school age have no schooling.

In the cities, education is better in middle- and upper-class neighbor-hoods. Students who complete nine years of elementary school may go to public secondary schools for three more years and then attend a university. El Salvador has three universities and several technical schools that prepare young people for careers in such fields as agriculture, communications, and engineering.

(Opposite) Hundreds of Roman Catholics carry the figure of Jesus Christ during a Palm Sunday procession in the town of Panchimalco. Religion is an important aspect of life in El Salvador. (Right) Soccer fans celebrate during a 2002 World Cup qualifying game in Cuscatlan Stadium, San Salvador. The national team is a source of pride to many Salvadorans.

5 El Salvador's Communities and Culture

DIFFERENCES IN INCOME lead to differences in how Salvadorans spend their leisure time. For most, recreation takes place in public places—on soccer fields, in marketplaces, or during religious festivals. For the wealthy, private clubs provide a range of entertainment. Even dress is different between city dwellers and those who live in the countryside. Uniting Salvadorans, however, is their music, literature, and for most, their religious faith.

The Family at the Center

The Salvadoran family has traditionally been at the center of Spanish-American culture. According to custom, families—usually including grand-

39

parents, aunts, uncles, and cousins—tended to be large and to live together under one roof. Married children who set up their own households usually did so in the same village or neighborhood as their parents.

Increasingly, common-law marriages, in which a couple lives together and raises a family without being legally married in a church or civil ceremony, occur in El Salvador and other poor Central American countries. About 70 percent of all children are born out of wedlock. Some parents who are unable to care for their children abandon them. El Salvador's orphanages—crowded during the civil war—are still bleak and underfunded.

Religion Brings Unity, Too

The Roman Catholic religion is an important part of El Salvador's Spanish heritage. Eighty-six percent of the population is Roman Catholic. The remaining Salvadorans are either Protestant, members of other faiths, or nonbelievers. Some country people, especially Amerindians, have blended the Catholic faith with practices of Amerindian faiths. They attend the Catholic mass, for instance, but bring baskets of corn to church to be blessed by the priest, just as their Mayan ancestors offered corn and other gifts to their gods. They sometimes pray to the ancient gods, too, for a good harvest, as well as to the Christian saints for blessings.

The Roman Catholic Church takes an active role in calling for social justice in El Salvador. Some priests met their deaths during the civil war because they criticized the government. By far the most famous among them was Archbishop Oscar Arnulfo Romero, who was assassinated in March 1980—the same month he was nominated for the Nobel Peace

A group of Roman Catholic students recreate the crucifixion of Jesus Christ on the streets of San Salvador. The students do this every year as part of the Holy Week celebration in the city. A large percentage of the population of El Salvador is either Roman Catholic or Protestant Christian.

Prize. Today, El Salvador's Catholic Church is unable to staff all of its parishes from the local population. Presently, about half of El Salvador's parishes are served by foreign priests, many of whom are Italians or Spaniards.

Protestant *sects* have won thousands of converts in recent years because they refuse to be drawn into politics. The Assemblies of God, the Seventh Day Adventists, the Church of God, and a few Pentecostal groups are all attracting increasing numbers of Salvadorans. Baptists, too, are

A food inspector checks the vegetables sold by vendors in a street market in El Salvador. The son of one of the vendors is sitting next to a basket of peppers.

active in El Salvador, with programs to help those in need of health care, housing, and food.

In some way, religion has a place in almost every Salvadoran's life. Some rural areas do not have churches, and traveling priests visit them only three or four times each year. In such villages, the priest's arrival signals a flurry of baptisms, confirmations, marriages, and funeral services. Missionary work by Protestant groups attracts hundreds to meetings and prayer services.

The biggest religious occasion each year—celebrated by most people regardless of their faith—is the fiesta, or feast, of the patron saint of each town or village. These saint's day fiestas often last as long as a week and include singing, dancing, lotteries, carnivals, flea markets, and dozens of parties. In some communities, societies called *confradía*, or religious brotherhoods, organize and pay for the fiestas with the help of townspeople who contribute money or their time.

Recreation and Leisure

Salvadorans work hard and enjoy time set aside for recreation and leisure. Watching and playing sports is a favorite form of recreation. Popular sports include soccer, softball, baseball, and basketball.

Salvadorans love to spend their leisure time outdoors. Many people play soccer, the national sport, in neighborhood fields. Soccer, called *futbol* in Spanish, is El Salvador's national sport, and it is played with passion. Soccer stadiums are found in nearly every city. From an early age, youngsters join school and neighborhood teams.

Many families spend their weekends at resorts near lakes or on the beaches along the Pacific Ocean. Throughout the country, the government has established a number of *turicentros*, or national recreational parks. One of the most beautiful and popular is Los Chorros, located near San Salvador. The park has four public swimming pools surrounded by tropical gardens and waterfalls.

San Jacinto Teleférico is an amusement park and entertainment complex on a mountain above San Salvador. Swiss-made cable cars carry visitors to the top, where they enjoy rides, games, music concerts, and folk dance performances. In San Salvador, children enjoy going to the Parque Infatil (Children's Park). The park includes a roller-skating rink, amusement rides, and boat rides on a small pond.

Most poor children have little time or energy for playing. When they do, they play games that do not require balls or jump ropes. With little money for toys, children make do with whatever they find—tin cans, sticks, stones, and bottles.

Many people listen to the radio several hours a day for entertainment and information. There are more than 100 commercial radio stations and one government-owned radio station. Eight commercial television stations cover the country, in addition to two government-owned and one church-based station. Most people in El Salvador do not own a television set, so they watch television at the village social club. The majority of shows are from the United States, with the dialogue *overdubbed* in Spanish.

The wealthy and middle-class have more time and money for leisure activities. They do much of their socializing at elegant private clubs. At sports clubs, members are offered fishing, tennis, golf, horseback riding, and water skiing. San Salvador has a few nightclubs and cocktail lounges with dinner and dancing, some of which require membership. The capital also boasts cinemas, some showing English-language films with subtitles, as well as dance halls and theatres.

Clothing: City Vs. County

For the most part, the wealthy and middle-class city dwellers of El Salvador wear the same kinds of clothing as people living in North American or Europe. When dressing formally women usually wear dresses and men suits. Women rarely wear pants, but jeans are popular among young men and women alike.

In the countryside, men wear hats to keep the sun off, usually large hats woven of palm leaves, with floppy brims. Country women wear ankle-length skirts and loose blouses, most often in dark colors. They often cover their heads with shawls or scarves if a stranger approaches. Most Salvadorans only have two or three changes of clothes, including one for special occasions.

Did You Know?

These are the official holidays in El Salvador. Other occasions are celebrated with parties and carnivals or family get-togethers. In addition, many towns hold a *festejo*, or festival, to honor its patron saint.

- January 1—New Year's Day
- March/April—Holy Week, Easter Sunday, Easter Monday
- May 1—Labor Day
- May 10—Mothers' Day
- July 19—National Liberation Day
- August 1 to 6—Festival El Salvador del Mundo
- September 15—Independence Day
- October 12—Columbus Day
- November 2—Day of the Dead
- December 24—Christmas Eve
- December 25—Christmas Day

Music and Literature

Before the Spanish conquest, music and art played an important part in the social and religious lives of the Indians. But Spanish conquerors destroyed many native art forms, replacing them with their own. As a result, very little is known about the pre-Columbian music of El Salvador. Most of what is known is based on archeological finds and performances by contemporary Indian music groups. Still, traces of Amerindian music have found their way into Salvadoran culture today. Wind and percussion instruments from the past can be heard, such as single- and multi-toned whistles called *pitos* that sound like flutes or piccolos. The *chirimia* has a reed mouthpiece and looks something like a clarinet. The most common percussion instruments are the *tambor* and *tun*. These large and small drums often accompany the *pito* and *chirmia* and the European guitar.

The most popular instrument, however, is the *marimba*, a xylophone made of wood. It originated in pre-Columbian Mexico and Guatemala, and was adopted as El Salvador's national instrument during the 20th century. As many as nine people can harmonize on the *marimba* keyboard, striking the gourds with padded sticks to produce delicate chimes. *Marimba* bands enliven every fiesta and wedding, and each year a *marimba* festival is held in San Miguel. Bands from all over the country set up their *marimbas* on the street corners, and people dance to the music.

(Opposite) A three-year-old girl shows off her traditional dress during a fiesta parade. The women who live in rural areas of El Salvador often wear dresses for special occasions.

Most Salvadoran literature has been written since its independence in 1821. Juan José Cañas is considered El Salvador's most famous romantic poet. He also wrote the lyrics to the national anthem. Francisco Antonio Gavidia, born in 1864, was perhaps the most important intellectual and writer of his time. His poem, "To Central America," condemns tyranny and proclaims his faith in democracy. His work, which includes several plays, is still widely read.

Manlio Argueta is probably El Salvador's best-known literary figure today. The novelist and poet was born in San Miguel in 1935. In an urgent and lively style, he writes of the lives and struggles of ordinary Salvadorans. Two of his critically acclaimed novels, *One Day of Life* and *Cuzcatlán*, have been translated into English. A champion for the rights of peasants, Argueta has been expelled from El Salvador four times for supporting various causes.

Simple Meals

Even Salvadoran children often eat a breakfast of coffee and bread. The people of El Salvador eat their largest meal in the middle of the day and often follow it with a siesta, or short nap. In the late afternoon or evening, those who can afford it have a snack or light meal. Sometimes this consists of a *papusa*, a Salvadoran specialty consisting of cornmeal cake stuffed with chopped meat and spices, which is sold in outdoor stalls. As in the days of the Mayas, hot chocolate is a favorite drink.

In the cities, there are numerous Chinese, Mexican, Italian, French, and local restaurants, plus several fast-food chains. The food market in San Salvador, one of the biggest and cleanest in Central America, has many stalls selling inexpensive food.

Tourist Attractions

El Salvador's balmy climate is ideal for enjoying open-air activities, such as tennis, golf, water skiing, surfing, fishing, swimming in the Pacific Ocean, or just lying on the unspoiled tropical beaches. Beautiful hotels line the beaches attracting tourists.

The capital, San Salvador, is a cosmopolitan city with modern hotels. The nightlife offers nightclubs and discotheques that attract people on vacation. Many restaurants offer international or quick American-style meals, traditional Salvadorean dishes, and a great variety of seafood.

Outside the cities, tourists tend to explore volcanoes, Mayan ruins, old colonial churches, colorful colonial markets, and Cerro Verde Park. *Ecotourism* businesses plan trips for tourists to waterfalls, river cascades, rainforests, and nature preserves.

El Salvadoran Festivals

The routine of daily life is often broken by special holidays and celebrations. Families and friends gather for weddings, birthdays, baptisms, and funerals. Most communities have their own carnivals and fiestas. These are celebrated by parades with colorful floats and costumes, fireworks, concerts, traditional folk dances, and athletic games. Vendors sell homemade food and handicrafts.

Most people get time off from work and school to observe official national holidays. September 15 is observed as Independence Day in El Salvador and the rest of Central America. A large military parade takes place, and family outings and picnics are popular.

Because El Salvador is mainly a Catholic nation, its most important holidays are religious in nature. El Salvador's most important national religious festival falls during the first week of August in honor of the Holy Savior of the World, "El Salvador," for whom the country is named. During this week, a wooden image of Jesus Christ, carved in 1777, is paraded through the streets of San Salvador to the National Palace and the cathedral, after which a band plays the national anthem. People flock to the capital city to enjoy the colorful processions, a large *feria* (fair), carnival rides, fireworks, soccer matches, and homemade foods.

The festival also includes special sporting events: soccer matches, bicycle races, and boxing matches. Carnivals do a thriving business. A local official crowns the Queen of the August Fair. Artists create artworks on sidewalks with dyed sawdust, similar to sand paintings made by Southwestern Indians in North America.

The two other weeklong celebrations are Holy Week and Christmas. During Christmas week, Salvadorans decorate their homes and churches with elaborate nativity scenes, called *nacimientos*. The scenes can take up an entire floor of a room and may include farms, villages, and roads leading to the manger. Some families may decorate a Christmas tree as well.

In addition, every town and city has its own patron saint, whose day is celebrated annually with a fiesta. The celebration helps keep local traditions alive. Fireworks and band concerts attract families. Children take a whack at piñatas, trying to break them. Usually made in the shape of animals from cardboard, paste, and colored paper, piñatas are filled with candy.

Non-religious festivals in El Salvador include the Sugar Cane Fair in Cojutepeque and the Street Festival of Ahuachapán in January; Flower Fiesta in Panchimalco in May; the July Festival in Santa Ana; the Balm Festival in Santa Tecla in October; the Straw Festival in Zacatecoluco; and Carnival in San Miguel in November.

A group of young men, representing Satan and called Talciguines, whip a man during Holy Week festivities in Texistepeque. The whipping represents the removal of the previous year's sins, while the ceremony as a whole symbolizes Jesus defeating the tempotations put before him by Satan.

Recipes

Pupusas

(Makes 25 pupusas)
1 pound vegetarian beef crumbles
1/2 large onion, finely diced
1 clove garlic, minced
1 medium fresh green pepper, seeded and minced
1 small tomato, finely chopped
1/2 teaspoon cumin
1/2 pound low-fat white cheese, grated
1/2 teaspoon salt
5 cups flour
4 cups water
1 teaspoon vegetable oil

Directions:

1. In a large, non-stick saucepan, over high heat, cook the vegetarian crumbles, onion, and garlic until cooked through. Reduce heat to low, and add the chili, tomato, and cumin. Let mixture cook until all liquid has evaporated. Set aside to cool. Stir in the cheese and salt.
2. Put the flour in a large mixing bowl, and stir in enough water to make a tortilla-like dough. Divide the dough into 25 pieces, and roll each into a ball. Flatten each ball between the palms of your hands to 1/2 inch. Put a spoonful of the meat mixture in the middle of each disk of dough, and enclose it firmly. Flatten the pupusas again until they are about 1/2 inch thick.
3. To cook, heat a flat, heavy-bottom skillet until it is hot. Brush the skillet with a little oil. Cook the pupusas on each side for four to five minutes until nicely browned. Serve warm by reheating slightly.

Arroz Con Leche

(Serves 4)
1/2 cup rice
1 stick cinnamon
2 cups water
1-1/2 c. sugar
4 cups milk
2 eggs, lightly beaten
2 tablespoons raisins

Directions:

1. Cook the rice for 15 minutes. Then, rinse in cold water and put into a pot with 2 cups water and cinnamon.
2. Cook over a medium flame until all the liquid has been absorbed. Reduce the heat, and add the sugar and the milk. Cook until the rice is done.
3. Add the eggs to the rice. Bring to a boil, then transfer at once to a serving dish and decorate with raisins.

Quesadilla Salvadorena

(Serves 8)
1 cup flour
1 cup sugar
1 cup sour cream
4 oz. Parmesan cheese (grated)
3 eggs
1 stick butter (small)
1 teaspoon baking powder
sesame seeds

Directions:

1. Preheat oven to 350° F.
2. Mix butter and sugar until creamy.
3. Add eggs one at the time.
4. Sift flour and baking powder. Add to sugar mixture little by little. Add sour cream and Parmesan cheese, mixing well.
5. Grease spring pan or baking dish with butter. Add mixture evenly. Decorate with sesame seeds.
6. Bake in preheated oven for 40 to 60 minutes.

Red Kidney Bean Soup

(Serves 4)
2 cups cooked red kidney beans
3 cups vegetable broth
2 tablespoons onion, chopped
1/2 cups whipping cream
Worcestershire sauce

Directions:

1. Put the cooked beans and the broth in a saucepan. Cook covered for 10 minutes and then let cool.
2. Liquefy in the blender, and pour into saucepan.
3. In a frying pan, sauté the onion until transparent.
4. Add onions to the soup, and cook 10 minutes more. Check seasoning, and sprinkle in some Worcestershire sauce. Before serving, add cream.

Pickled Cabbage El Salvador Style

(Serves 6)
1 small head green cabbage, cored and sliced very thin
1 small red onion, sliced thin
1 medium carrot, pared and cut into very thin circles
1 cup diced fresh pineapple
1-1/2 teaspoons minced garlic
1/2 cup white vinegar
1/2 cup pineapple juice
Salt and pepper to taste

Directions:

Combine all ingredients, and mix well. Cover. Refrigerate overnight, stirring occasionally. Will keep, covered and refrigerated, about four days.

Glossary

Catastrophe—a violent, usually destructive, natural event.

Communistic—favoring a government-controlled society in which all property is shared.

Conquistadors—leaders of the Spanish conquest of America.

Drought—a long period without rain.

Ecotourism—a form of tourism that strives to minimize ecological or other damage to areas visited for their natural or cultural interest.

Exile—forced absence from one's home or country.

Export—a commodity conveyed from one country or region to another for purpose of trade.

Federation—a union of groups.

Free trade—trade based on unrestricted exchange of goods with tariffs (taxes) only used to create revenue, not keep out foreign goods.

Geological—having to do with the earth's structure.

Guerrilla—a person who is part of an irregular army and uses tactics of sabotage.

Import—merchandise brought in from another country.

Indigo—a blue dye made from plants.

Isthmus—a narrow strip of land connecting two larger land areas.

Junta—a group controlling a government after taking it over.

Magnitude—great size or amount.

Nomadic—roaming.

Overdub—to add a second layer of sound or music to a recording.

Plantation—a large estate or farm where crops such as coffee, bananas, cotton, or rubber trees are grown, usually worked by resident laborers.

Plateau—a level land area raised sharply above nearby land on at least one side.

Preserve—an area set aside for the protection and preservation of plants and animals.

Province—an administrative district or division of a country.

Reform—to improve by removing old faults or inequities.

Republican—a representative form of government.

Richter scale—a scale for measuring the severity of earthquakes created by Charles F. Richter.

Sect—a dissenting religious body.

Slum—a crowded city area with unsanitary, run-down housing.

Sorghum—a tropical grass similar to Indian corn.

Subsistence—minimum needed to sustain life.

Tectonic—having to do with the crust of a planet, its faults and folds.

Vegetation—plant life.

Project and Report Ideas

Maps and Posters

- Make a relief map using water, flour, and watercolor paints showing the three landscapes of El Salvador (see Chapter One). Mix the flour and water into a thick dough that you can shape on a 1/2-inch piece of wood (particle board is inexpensive and works well). Allow your model of El Salvador to dry thoroughly before painting it. Include a legend to indicate the colors for water, coast land, plateau, and so on.
- Make a poster showing the steps in growing, harvesting, and processing coffee. Most people don't know how coffee arrives in their local supermarket.

Flashcards

Using the glossary in this book, create flashcards. Put the term on one side and the definition on the other. Practice with the cards in pairs. Then, choose two teams of three. Select a referee to say the term out loud, and then call on someone to give the definition. The referee's decision is final. Award points for each correct answer. You can also read the definition, and ask for the correct term instead!

Projects

- Make a piñata— find a picture of one to use as a model.
- Choose either the plants or animals of El Salvador and make mobiles of them to hang in class.
- Make a cutaway model of a volcano, showing its interior.

Research Report

In teams, assemble a list of the best Web sites for finding out about El Salvador. Devise a rating system. Include a one- or two-sentence summary about the site. Combine these sites into a comprehensive guide to El Salvador on the Internet for other classes to use.

"Cost of Living" Project

Many Salvadoran families live on $10 a day. Figure out how much your family lives on a day. To calculate this, you must find out or estimate the costs of these items or resources your family uses every day:

Food ____ (Divide monthly cost by 30.)

Electricity ____ (Divide your parents' monthly bill by 30.)

Gas ____ (Use the same method as for electricity.)

Water ____ (Use the same method as for electricity.)

Health insurance ____ (Ask your parents for an estimate, and divide by 365 days.)

Education ____ (Find out from the principal's office how much in tax dollars is spent on each student at your school per year. Divide by 183 school days. Multiply by the number of school-age children in your family.)

Total the amount. How many people in El Salvador could support themselves on the costs tied to you each day? Show your research as a chart. Add a paragraph at the end explaining your thoughts about the results.

Classroom Fiesta

If your city, town, or village was going to have an annual festival that captured some of the best things about where you live, what should be included? In small groups, choose examples of:

- Local, popular, or traditional food
- Local or regional music (country/western, jazz, religious, etc.)
- Exhibitions of local crafts or hobbies (fishing, soccer, baseball, gardening, etc.)
- Displays of symbols in your area: the city seal, the school mascot, the mascot of the favorite professional sports team, the religious symbols used outside of churches and temples, etc.
- Illustrations of native wildlife—commonly seen plants and animals

57

Chronology

1500 B.C.	Native civilizations in El Salvador most likely begin.
A.D. 1100	Two large Amerindian states and several smaller ones flourish in the region, populated mainly by the Pipils.
1522	A Spanish ship's officer leads an expedition to Meanguera Island, located in the Gulf of Fonseca.
1524	Spanish captain Pedro de Alvarado arrives, prepared for conquest, but is defeated.
1525	De Alvarado returns, this time succeeding in conquering the tribes.
1811	A brief revolution flares up against Spain, but fails.
1821	All Central American countries, including El Salvador, declare independence from Spain.
1850s	Coffee as a crop is introduced in El Salvador, later becoming the center of the economy.
1900-30	El Salvador experiences a long period of stability.
1932	Conservative military officers succeed in toppling the reformist government. After executing communist revolutionary leader Faribundo Martí, they ordered what became known as *La Matanza* (the massacre), the slaughter of some 10,000 Pipil Indians suspected of sympathizing with Martí. This event strongly influences El Salvador's later history.
1969	El Salvador and Honduras fight the 100-hour Soccer War over border disputes.
1972	Opponents of military rule unite under Jose Napoleon Duarte; he is defeated in the presidential election by widespread fraud, and is later exiled.

1979	Guerrilla warfare is widespread throughout the country.
1982	Salvadorans elect a new assembly; power is peacefully transferred to a civilian president.
1983	The Legislative Assembly drafts a new constitution establishing a republican government and strengthening individual rights.
1984	Duarte wins the presidential election, becoming the first freely elected president in 50 years.
1989	Alfredo Cristiani wins the presidency, the first time power has passed from one freely elected civilian president to another; Cristiani calls for peace talks with rebel guerrillas.
1991	El Salvadoran government and the rebels sign the New York City Accord as a first step toward peace.
1992	The two sides sign the Accords of Chapultepec in Mexico City, finalizing the peace.
1998	Hurricane Mitch strikes El Salvador, flooding thousands of acres of farmland and killing 374 people.
1999	39-year-old Francisco Flores Perez is selected as president of El Salvador, becoming the youngest man to be elected to the office.
2001	The U.S. dollar becomes legal currency in El Salvador.
2002	Latin American leaders, including President Francisco Flores Perez, meet in Argentina for the Global Alumni Conference to discuss technological and economic issues.

Further Reading/Internet Resources

Argueta, Jorge. *A Movie in My Pillow*. San Francisco: Children's Book Press, 2001.

Bachelis, Faren Maree. *El Salvador*. Chicago: Childrens Press, 1990.

Foley, Erin. *El Salvador*. New York: Marshall Cavendish, 1995.

Henderson, James D. *A Reference Guide to Latin American History*. Armonk, N.Y.:
    M. E. Sharpe, 2000.

Saunders, Renfield. *El Salvador*. New York: Chelsea House, 1998.

Towell, Larry and Mark Danner. *El Salvador*. New York: W. W. Norton, 1997.

Woodward, Ralph Lee Jr. *Central America: A Nation Divided*, 3rd ed. New York: Oxford
    University Press, 1999.

Travel information

http://www.travel-guide.com/data/slv/slv070.asp
http://www.abest.com/~rlba1/English.htm
http://www.state.gov/www/background_notes/elsal_0008_bgn.html

History and Geography

http://www.infoplease.com/ipa/A0107489.html
http://lanic.utexas.edu/region/central.html

Economic and Political Information

http://www.odci.gov/cia/publications/factbook/geos/es.html
http://www.atlapedia.com/online/countries/elsalvad.htm
http://lcweb2.loc.gov/frd/cs/svtoc.html

Culture and Festivals

http://www.lonelyplanet.com/destinations/central_america/el_salvador/
http://www.britannica.com/eb/article?eu=118707

Caribbean/Latin American Action
1818 N Street NW, Suite 310
Washington, D.C. 20036
(202) 466-7464

Embassy of the Republic of El Salvador
Ambassador Rene Antonio Leon
    Rodriguez
2308 California Street NW
Washington, D.C. 20008
(202) 265-9671

**Embassy of the United States
in El Salvador**
Ambassador Anne W. Patterson
Final Boulevard Santa Elena, Antiguo
Cuscatlan, San Salvador
Unit 3116, APO AA 34023
(503) 278-4444

U.S. Department of Commerce
International Trade Administration
Office of Latin America and the Caribbean
14th and Constitution Avenue NW
Washington, D.C. 20230
(202) 482-1658
(800) USA-TRADE
Website address: http://www.ita.doc.gov

Index

Contributors

Senior Consulting Editor **James D. Henderson** is professor of
international studies at Coastal Carolina University. He is the
author of *Conservative Thought in Twentieth Century Latin America:
The Ideals of Laureano Gómez* (1988; Spanish edition *Las ideas de
Laureano Gómez* published in 1985); *When Colombia Bled: A History
of the Violence in Tolima* (1985; Spanish edition *Cuando Colombia se
desangró, una historia de la Violencia en metrópoli y provincia*, 1984);
and co-author of *A Reference Guide to Latin American History*
(2000) and *Ten Notable Women of Latin America* (1978).

   Mr. Henderson earned a bachelors degree in history from Centenary College of
Louisiana, and a masters degree in history from the University of Arizona. He then
spent three years in the Peace Corps, serving in Colombia, before earning his doctorate
in Latin American history in 1972 at Texas Christian University.

Charles J. Shields, the author of all eight books in the
DISCOVERING CENTRAL AMERICA series, lives in Homewood, a
suburb of Chicago, with his wife Guadalupe, an elementary-
school principal. He has a degree in history from the University
of Illinois in Urbana-Champaign, and was chairman of the
English department and the guidance department at
Homewood-Flossmoor High School in Flossmoor, Illinois.